THERE'S A
MESSAGE
IN YOUR
MESS

THERE'S A MESSAGE IN YOUR MESS

RIA CLARK

"A professional writer is an amateur who didn't quit."

Contents

Special Dedication

I am dedicating this book to and in memory of my mentor, my coach, my therapist, my sister, my breastie, and my friend:

Michelle ChellyRey Reynolds

I am having a hard time trying to process that you are no longer here with me. Michelle, you made me feel like I was your only friend. You would always call, text, message, and Marco Polo me every other day since the day we met. I have only known you throughout my breast cancer journey, but no one can tell me God did not place you in my life when I needed you most.

We shared our ups and downs on this journey. Sometimes we laughed and sometimes we cried, but you always reminded me, we were special. God chose US to go through this journey for a reason. God had US on a special assignment. When I would start feeling down about my journey, I would go to you. You would remind me why I was going through this journey. Who will I talk to now? I know you are in a better place and there is no more pain, but I wish God would have given me a little more time with you.

I watched one of your Marco Polos. You always greeted me saying, "Heeeeeeeyyyyy Sis!" You were so proud and excited about my book coming out. It is because of you I finally finished this book. I am so glad you got a chance to read it.

No one wants to be a part of this group called Cancer, but because of Cancer I met you. The hardest part about being a member of this group is that you are faced with death constantly. You must look death in the face more than once.

One thing about you, you did not fear death. Your faith in God was so strong and amazing. Your talks would comfort my soul. With the little time here on earth, you have accomplished more than someone who is still here. You were a daughter, sister, mother, wife, cousin, friend, author, minister, entrepreneur, founder, and co-founder of different organizations and most important a child of God.

One thing I know for sure that you loved more than anything was your family and friends. You were a daddy's girl, just like me and momma's baby. Your husband and your children were your world. You had a heart of gold and a beautiful smile that would just light up the room. When I was having a hard time dealing with my journey you always told me at the end of our serious conversations that, "Everything may work out, but maybe not, but always trust God."

That reminds me how your love for God was a perfect love story. I knew no matter what happened to you, God was in control, and you were ok with His decision. You would love God and give Him the praise no matter what. The type of mindset you had speaks volumes. The type of relationship that you had with God, I strive to achieve in my life. Thank you, for the blueprint.

I just want to thank God for allowing YOU to be a part of my life. Things happen for a reason and a season. I will never forget you; you have no idea how many times you turned my tears into laughter. May your soul sleep eternally in God's arms

Love you Breastie, Sister, and Friend

To My Children

Quenton and Jaylen, you are my why and the reason I fought so hard at this thing called life. God blessed me with you, and I am so honored to be your mother. You boys are the best thing that ever happened to me.

Quenton, you were my first born, and the first time I saw your face, I could not believe God blessed me with such a beautiful baby. You are so much like me; it is a blessing and a curse. My prayer for you is that you stay focused on your dreams and aspirations. Put God first, and before you make any drastic decision in life, make sure you pray about it first. Always know I love you just the way you are. I would not change anything about you. When I look at you, I am so proud of you. I cannot wait for the world to hear your voice. You are not just my son, but you are my best friend. Love you!!!

Jaylen, you are my baby, and I could not believe I was gonna be a mother again. You are so much like me it is scary. You are sensitive, yet strong.

Growing up, I love the fact that you always wanted to be around me and needed me for everything. You made sure when you wanted my attention you would get it. I am so proud of the man you are becoming. My prayer for you is to stay focused and to set goals for yourself, then achieve them. It is time to grow up and see what the world has to offer. You will be just fine; your daddy and I will be with you every step of the way. Put God first and pray before making any decisions in life. You are not just my son, but you are my best friend. Love you!!!

Introduction

Tuesday, November 19, 2019
Twelve O'clock Noon

This book is about my life! One of my best friends (Julie Wilson) told me a long time ago, "Life is simple; we make it complicated." With that being said, God gave us a free will a long time ago. It is up to us which choices we are going to make. We will make some good ones and some bad ones. We just have to hope and pray.

When we make a choice, we must deal with the consequences – good or bad. Life did not come with a guide to follow. Life is based on our foundation that was prepared for us before we were even born.

The foundation of life is the Bible. That is why God gave us parents, grandparents, and so forth – so that they can be examples to the children – to help them grow up to be productive people in this world. Right? Well, everyone that is born is not fortunate enough to have both parents and have the same opportunities.

Some people come from a lot of bad situations, and I cannot even name them all, but I will try. Teenage pregnancy, rape, molestation, infidelity, religion, death, and the list can go on. So, you say, "What do those people do and how will they get their guidance to succeed at this thing called life?" Good questions. My book is designed to reveal how our mess becomes our message.

"No matter who you are,
no matter what you did,
no matter where you are from,
you can always change and become
a better version of yourself."

Chapter 1

WHERE ARE YOU FROM?

We have to first start here, "Where did we come from?" That means, "Who are our parents and grandparents? Where does our history start?" It is especially important to know these answers and have these conversations. It helps to shape our identity to know who we are and what to expect as we go through this thing called life. We have to ask questions about mental health, physical health, traditions, religion, and my favorite – the stories.

For me, growing up my parents were married, and I had the experience of being in a household with both parents. From what I can remember, we had some great times. I experienced having my own room. It was decorated with my favorite cartoon character (Strawberry Short-cake). My mom took me places, like New York, to see *The Wiz*, she put me in ballet, dance, piano (I can only play "Frog in the Pond") and tap dance. I can remember never wanting to take off my black-and-white body suit. It had feathers and rhinestones, my shoes were shiny, and they made noise, so I would tap dance all over the house.

Mom was amazing. She was a hard worker. She took care of the house, loved to shop, cook, bake, and loved to dance. We had the best house parties. I would sit on the step and watch her and my dad dance. Sometimes, she would run me back upstairs and sometimes she would let me dance with her and dad. Now, what I did not like is the fact that I had a bedtime. I would miss FAME (the TV show), but every now and then mom would let me stay up and watch it.

She was big on discipline, and she did not tolerate back talk. She started early on teaching me respect and obedience. I caught on quickly because even at that early age, I was totally scared of her.

My dad was the pushover. I could fuss at him about everything and he would never fuss at me unless it was necessary. He did not let things get to him, at least that is how I thought of him. If he had stuff going on, I did not know it.

We lived in D.C. at the time, and it gets cold there. I could not understand why dad would let mom take the good car with the heat.

Not knowing, he was showing me that a man is supposed to sacrifice for his wife and make sure she has what she needs. But I was like, "I'm a child . . . I need heat." Nonetheless, she put me in the cold car with dad, but he worked closer to my school, so it made sense. Not knowing then, I would be doing this same thing with my kids.

I would fuss at him, and he would never say a word. He would look at me and shake his head. Dad was a great provider. He worked hard. He was in the military and made sure we had everything we needed. He loved road trips. He loved house parties. He loved to fry chicken, and my personal favorite was his fried pork chops. He was an organizer, which drove me crazy sometimes.

To me, my parents were the perfect match. They looked good together. I never saw them argue and they always did things together and with me. Then, something major happened in life. My mom told me she was pregnant with my brother. I was happy at first, until his arrival.

The family would come over and walk right past me to see him. I remember sitting on the step and mom came and sat by me. She told me everyone still loved me, but they were excited for him because he was new and fresh. She made me get off the step and took me over to the family, and they embraced me, too. They would say, "Look at your little brother," and I would kiss him and hold him from time to time. He would get on my nerves with that crying and mom would say I had to take care of the baby.

My time with her was getting shorter by the day. I did not understand, at the time, what that meant. All I knew was he was getting all the attention I used to get. I remember one night when everybody was asleep, I went in his room, and I tore the ear of his Snoopy! I guess I felt like I was getting him because he took my mommy.

Early childhood is particularly important for kids because I started developing my own personality. Based on my experiences, the seed was planted, and my mom and dad were fertilizing me. They could only instill in me what they knew from their upbringing. With what I had seen was it right or wrong? Who is to say? For me, as a child, I was happy until . . . the divorce.

"Spouses may divorce but parents are parents forever."

Chapter 2

THE DIVORCE

I thought everything was fine and good. We were living our best lives until one day my mom came to me. I was about seven or eight years old and she told me we were moving to Florida. She and dad were separating. My heart dropped. I still remember that feeling. The two people who were my heroes were parting ways. Where was I going? Why did I have to leave my big house, my friends, and my family?

I cannot quite remember if we flew or drove to Florida because we took road trips all the time. I knew both of my parents were from Sanford, Florida. I always loved to hear their love story, but I did not know much about my family at that age, only via phone calls and holidays. My dad was in the military, stationed in Guam, where I was born, so I was a little excited to see my family. At that time, my grandparents were living, except my mom's dad. He passed when I was three.

We went to Florida and we stayed with my Aunty Margaret first, then my Aunty Faye. I got a chance to spend a lot of time with my cousins, whom I call my sisters, now - Nicole Lemon and Terriashi Cashe. We have made some great memories together. They were the sisters I always wanted. We would stay over each other's house. We played together. We went to school together. We told each other secrets. We fought. We laughed. We cried. We did not talk to each other when we were mad, but I am glad I grew up with them.

My mother and father did not get a divorce right away, but when they finally did, it changed me. Our whole way of living changed. I will not say it was bad, but different. I was used to certain things, and we had what we needed but not what we wanted some of the time. There was a difference. My brother did not notice it because he was so young, but I did!

My mom's whole attitude changed once dad was gone for good. Divorce is not hard on the husband and wife; it is hard on the kids, too. My life changed. I missed my dad through all the monumental moments in my life because we were in two different states. Now, let me be clear-he was there for me and did the best he could do. Despite the odds, both of my parents were honest, truthful, and never sugarcoated anything. They may not have told me everything, but I was very clear on what was going on.

My whole view on marriage changed. Now, I was worried if I got married, would my marriage end in divorce, too. I had so many questions because I did not know what happened. How could two people I never saw argue or fight get divorced? At that time, I figured divorce was bad. Remember, the seed was planted. My parents were fertilizing me. They could only teach me what they knew. As a result, my way of thinking was already changing.

Often, I found myself pondering, *was it for the better or worse*? Remember, as parents, when we make major decisions, they do not only affect us but the little people that look up to us. They are watching everything we do. We must be incredibly careful about what we expose our kids to because at that age, 10 or 11, even at 45 years old, I remember things – clear and in color, like it was yesterday.

"Where you come from does not determine where you are going."

Chapter 3

NEW BEGINNINGS

A few years passed and we were in our new house. I had started middle school and I was trying to figure out who I was trying or wanted to be. My mom had picked up a second job, and I had to take care of my little brother until she got home. I still did what kids do. I played outside, talked on the phone, watched TV, listened to music, did homework, chores, and loved fashion even as a young lady. I liked boys, but I was not quite into them like that, just yet. At this point in my life, I liked clothes, shoes, jewelry, getting my hair done, and just hanging with my friends. Let Nikki tell it, I had a new best friend every week! I always thought I was cute!

Our house would get broken into at least once a week. My mom was in one room and my brother and I were in another. One night, we were in bed for the night. I felt a light breeze in the room. I went to turn over. Mind you, my eyes were still closed. Frantically, I was woken up by a strange man with his hands over my mouth. I could not scream, but I started kicking and fighting. I do not know where my strength came from, but I threw him off me. He was standing in the corner of the room. He was telling me to be quiet by putting his hands over his mouth. He was saying, "Sheeeshhh." I screamed so loud that my brother woke up and just looked, so I started picking up stuff to throw at the man. He reached over and tried to grab my brother, so I snatched my brother and ran to the door, but because we had so many break-ins, I had put the dresser against the door.

It felt like I was in slow motion. I could not move that dresser fast enough. My brother was standing next to me and we were trying to get out of that room. He (the intruder) jumped out the window. When I got the door opened, my mom was standing there with her pistol and ran outside and started shooting.

My momma was so mad that she forgot that me and my brother were standing there. She turned around and said, "Oh my God!" She looked like something clicked in her mind saying, "Your kids!" She started apologizing and hugging us. She called the police and she called this man she had been seeing. His name was Billy Raines. He would come by the house from time to time, but he did not live with us. He was a nice guy, and he was there helping with the police. He walked up to me, gave me a hug, and said, "This will never happen again." He moved in a few weeks later.

That was the first time I ever saw so many police at one time talking to me, my mom, and Billy. They took prints. They had gloves on. It was a mess. I remember my mom calling my dad because over the years, they got along for us. If they had issues, I did not know. I talked to my dad and told him everything. I was so shaken up my mom let me stay home from school that day.

I remember being so scared, yet I gathered enough courage to walk outside and look on the ground where the robber jumped out the window. I saw footprints going toward the house next door and I followed them as much as I could, but they started fading. I knew from that day, it had to be someone from next door, or he probably ran that way to get away quicker because we had an open field in the front of our house. The seed was planted. My parents were fertilizing me. But now, I was thinking different about people and fear.

"I truly believe that one virtuous young woman led by the spirit can change the world."

Chapter 4

SHE'S A YOUNG LADY

You may be wondering, *where is she going with her story*? Well, I am telling you my story because it is important for you to know how I became the woman I am today: it was my life experiences and the choices I made. My seed was broken and now I was growing. With every experience I was going through at this point, it was to see what type of woman I would become. These were my leaves blossoming on the tree. I had to take what I had been taught, what I had seen, and what I had known (based on my experiences) to find my true self. Did I like some of the decisions I made? Of course not, but it was my truth and my choice.

By now, I was a senior in high school, and I was living my best life. I had two jobs and a couple of boyfriends. I was preparing for college. I was sick of Sanford. The town was too small for me. I could not do "nothing" or go anywhere because everybody knew my mom and dad. Even when I would get in trouble, they would say, "Oh, you're a Cherry or Clark." That drove me crazy, so I told my CMS sisters - Latisha Jerrells (Howard), Kateria Barfield (Simmons), Katrina Ransome, Xavier Sessions (Williams), Lakeshia Coleman (Hunter), Chandreka Newkirk, Sanquita Brooks, and Regina Smith, that when I graduated I was moving to Washington, D.C. CMS stands for "Cash Money Sisters." We got it from New Jack City – for the 90's babies! They would laugh, but they knew what I meant. I would tell them all the time, "I can't do this small town." I told my dad, "I want to come there and go to college." He said, "Ok."

I graduated high school on June 5, 1992 and was in D.C. August 5, 1992. I was not playing. I was ready to go, plus my mom wanted me to go away to college. Well, to my surprise, when it was time to leave to go to D.C. with my dad, I found out I was pregnant. Yes, y'all – pregnant! So, I did not want to go to D.C. and lie to my dad. I told him before we left in case he said I could not come. My dad and I always had great, open communication. I was not going to ruin that because my dad was always fair, and I knew he would not get mad.

I remember telling him and he dropped his head. He said, "Ok, let's just get to D.C. and we will figure it out when we get there." I was happy because he did not leave me. I kissed everybody goodbye, and on the road, we went, not realizing I had a major decision I would have to make once I got to D.C.

One day, I was in my room at my dad's house. He and my bonus mom asked me to come downstairs to the basement. I came down all happy and jolly. My bonus mom had taken me shopping for a nice coat and then they dropped a bomb on me. They told me I had to decide that day if I was going to school or going to be a mom. This was the first time I heard about abortion. They gave me the pros and cons and, I chose abortion.

Let me be clear, they did not force me to do it. I made the choice on my own. Today, my child would have been 25 years old. I think about that from time to time. Do I regret it? No, because I thought I was too young to have a baby. I will always remember that day! I will forever be grateful for my older cousin, Bridgette. She was there with me from the beginning to the end. That was a decision I would soon have to pay for and be reminded about.

I do not regret any decisions I have made in life, but I would have done some things differently, but no regrets. After that abortion, I never looked at men the same. Remember, God already has our lives planned out as sure as we live and as sure as we die. My parents planted the seed and had released me in the garden. My flower was blooming. All things in between would be because of me.

"She's a strong cup of black coffee in a world that is drunk on the cheap wine of shallow love."

Chapter 5

COLLEGE GIRL

My first day of school. The school was right down the street from my dad's house, and I was so excited! I was single and was moving on with the choice I made. I accomplished one of my goals, to leave Sanford and go to school. I attended Prince George Community College in Largo, Maryland. My major was Respiratory Therapy, but once I got to Howard University, I changed my major to Physical Therapy.

It was definitely a great experience. College was nothing like high school. I stayed skinny back then because the classes were far away, and I had to walk to every class. One thing I did like, I could pick my own schedule, so I went to morning classes and would do my lab, then go to my afternoon classes. I had professors and they gave me a syllabus, and that was how I did my assignments and homework. I grew up fast in college. It made me responsible and accountable.

I met my first best friend, Dionne, in college. Dionne was my tour guide for the DMV. She showed me how to catch the bus, catch the subway, and all the ins-and-outs about DMV. We had good times together. We met celebrities. We went to concerts, met boys, went to plays, clubs, parties, trips, shopping sprees, and had the time of our lives. My dad was in the picture, so he still would drop us off and pick us up from everywhere. He would just shake his head, never complaining. When I think about the stuff we did, we should not be alive. It was by God's grace we are still here. We did some reckless stuff and had so much fun doing it.

We did everything together, and when we would plan things, they would never go as planned. We called that our "Ria and Dionne's Adventures." That was the best time of my life. I was dating, hanging out, going out of town, had moved into my first apartment, had no kids, was working two jobs, and was going to school. Dionne got a car first, and then it was on! We have some stories that we will probably take to our grave.

I also experienced my first heartbreak in college. After that, it was on! I was a whore for about two years, and I loved every minute of it, and I would not change a thing about it –

PERIOD! Ladies, the men get a whore phase – so should we. It does not last as long as the men, but every woman needs to go through a whore phase.

Dionne and I were inseparable for about four years straight, until I got pregnant, again. I lost touch with Dionne because I did not know how to separate the two. I chose a man over my friend (first grown woman mistake I made). That relationship was the most toxic relationship I had ever been in – very verbally, mentally, and physically abusive. That is when the cycle of choosing toxic men in my life became a never- ending cycle. I dropped out of college, after being accepted into the physical therapy program, because I was pregnant. I ended up getting a job at the University. I tried to go back, but having a baby was hard. I kept telling myself *I am going to go back*. Here I am, over 25 years later, with no degree (another bad choice and grown woman mistake; I should have stayed in school).

That was the cycle of starting stuff but never completing anything. My flower was still blooming. The leaves were getting green. The plant was growing up. A few leaves had fallen off, but it still was growing and was still being watered.

"Home is where the heart is."

Chapter 6

GOING BACK HOME

My breakup with my oldest son's father was hurtful, and this was a different type of relationship for me because I could not just walk away and forget he ever existed. I had to continue to deal with him because I had a baby with him. In my previous relationships, it was easy to break up because afterwards, we were done. I did not have to deal with them anymore, so I would go on with my life.

Let me tell you, be careful who you have your kids from because you are tied to them for the rest of your life. He was so evil and mean! I was so sick of the toxic behavior and relationship that I packed up my stuff and went back to Florida.

Motherhood was hard for me, so I needed a break and a get-away. I asked my son's grandmother if she could keep my son until I got to Florida and got settled. Then, I would come back to get him. Let me tell you about my son's grandmother. Ms. Evelyn was the most beautiful person I had known. She treated me like I was her daughter. She was there for me from the moment I met her, and when I got pregnant with my oldest son, we became very close. She knew what I was going through with my son's father, and I had fallen into a deep depression. I had gained weight, loss my job, had another failed relationship, and had a baby on top of all of that. As a result, I was not feeling too good about myself. I needed to go home, be with my mother, and figure this thing called "life" out because now it was not just me anymore; it was me and my son.

I went home for a year. I stayed with my mom and Billy (my bonus dad). I went to school. I worked two jobs and I was trying to better myself. I went back to a relationship that failed the first time. I should have learned from that situation: you never go back to a relationship when trust and loyalty are broken. Nonetheless, I had the tendency of going back to situations that were familiar and comfortable. In hindsight, I learned from that relationship once I am done to never go back. When I did, their actions proved that they did not love or care about me. They thought, *Yes, I got her, and she is never going to leave. She will always come back, so I can treat her the way I want to.* Negative! I am not saying all relationships are that way, but I am speaking for me. This relationship was easier for me to walk away from because I had no ties with this person. So, it was easier to move on and forget about that relationship for GOOD!

Like yesterday, I remember when my mom, my aunt, and I went to North Carolina to get my son. When I saw him, he was a year old, and they had cut his hair. He was the cutest thing I ever saw. I could not believe I had a part in creating this amazing little boy. He would not come to me at first, but after talking to him and apologizing, he finally came to me, and we were inseparable from that day forward.

We stayed for the family reunion, we laughed and played before we hit the road to go back to Florida to start our new life. I was still working two jobs and going to school. I put Quenton in daycare. I was living with my mom and Billy. They were helping me with Quenton. Billy loved Quenton. He would spend time with him, taking him places. Quenton loved bath time with him. He would sing to him. Every time he would dress Quenton, he would put so much powder in his diaper that Quenton would be running around the house with a trail of baby powder following behind him!

I was happy being home with my parents. I got to see my favorite cousin ("sis."), Nikki and hang out with her a little. Even though she was back and forth from college, we did get a chance to hang out. I missed being with her. Our conversations were always good – to the point we would talk into the early hours of the morning – falling asleep together on the couch. We still do that sometimes.

My CMS sisters and I would hang out, as well. With them, it was like old times. I did not realize how much I missed them until I could no longer see them. Whether they knew it or not, I always prayed for them, and from time to time, I would chat with them and catch up on life. Being friends with them was the foundation of sisterhood. They taught me the real meaning of friendship and sisterhood. I love those ladies with every breath in me. We created the blueprint to friendship because nothing was perfect about it, but at the end of the day we were perfect for each other. We are sisters to this day, over 25 years of friendship.

I got a chance to spend time with my family and be there for the get-togethers we always had growing up. My Aunt Joyce's house was the spot. We hung out, laughed, ate, and simply enjoyed each other's company. If I wanted to see a relative, I had not seen in a long time, I would go over Aunty Joyce's or Aunty Margaret's. That was the place to be. Once my grandmother passed away, Aunty Joyce took over watching over the family. She reminds me so much of my grandmother – giving and sweet. I love her cooking and I love her stories about the family and her life. Aunty Joyce let us do whatever we wanted. I loved going over her house as a child and as an adult.

After a few months, Quenton got extremely sick, with a high fever and came down with this virus. I cannot remember what it was called, but basically, he could not live in Florida because his body could not deal with the heat. I reached out to his father, and we talked. He wanted me to come back to Maryland, so we could try and be a family. I knew that was not a good idea because I said, "I would never go back to that relationship." However, in my mind, I thought, "Well, this is my child's father; this time it will be different." I was wrong.

This is what I mean about choices. I knew in my mind it was a horrible idea, but in my heart, I thought it would be better for my son. My flower in the garden was blooming because I was finally finding myself again and loving myself. I had loss some weight, I was being a good mother, and I was making some accomplishments. Yet because of a man, I allowed my vision to become cloudy. *My poor garden*, I exhaled. *"I do not know how many times I can keep bringing you back to life. Did I make the right decision going back to D.C.?*

"Stop trying to repair your heart by putting it back into the hands that broke it"

Chapter 7

WE'LL TRY THIS AGAIN

After saying my good-byes, we drove to Florida with my son and all my belongings. When I got there, I had to stay with Ms. Evelyn, so I could get back on my feet. Ms. Evelyn was a joy to be around. She always had my best interest at heart. She was like a second mother. She did not play about her family.

Living in her house was a little challenging at times. It felt like I was going backwards. I had a child, and I was ready to be in my own place. After a few weeks of staying there, my son's father started acting funny. He became distant, walking pass me like I did not exist. I would hear him on the phone talking to other women. I was thinking, *I fell for his crap and he probably had no intentions of getting back with me*. So, I asked him what was wrong because I thought we were trying to work on our relationship. He said, "I told you that so you could bring my son home. I never had any intentions of getting back with you." Then, he walked away. That was another bad decision and choice I made.

I continued to stay with Ms. Evelyn while I tried to find a job to move out. I reconnected with Dione and bought her old car, and I found a job working in downtown D.C. I was excited about this job because I always wanted to work in downtown D.C. like my mom and stepmom. I loved seeing them get dressed for work. I would think, "When I grow up, I want to be just like them." When I would go downtown, I would see the women with their business suit, leather briefcase, classic white Reebok tennis shoes, and their faces would beat to the gods. I thought to myself, *that is the type of woman I want to be – a career woman*.

I met some amazing people at my new job, and I started dating a little, but these men were all crazy and full of themselves. The men were different in D.C. I was not accustomed to, nor was I in the business of taking care of men. Where I come from, the men were supposed to take care of the women. Growing up in the south, you were taught that at an early age. I had also seen that growing up with my father and stepdad as they took care of the house. They made sure we had what we needed as a family.

It was really hard dating after everything I had been through, but at that age, I felt I needed a man in my life. So, can you imagine what happened when I started to feel that way? I started thinking, *I can at least get that – a man. At least he got a job. At least, he got all his hair and teeth. At least, he got a piece of a car. He stays with his momma. That is ok. He loves her and is helping her."* This is where I went wrong. Most of the men I dated, I knew they were no good – but at least, I had a piece of a man – because that is all it was.

After all I tried to do to rebuild my life again, I started failing. I tried to lose weight, be a good mother, find a new man, keep my good job, get me a new car, and find an apartment for my son and me. I knew one thing I was going to do and that was take a break from dating these raggedy men. Well, at least, that was what I thought.

I was going to lunch one day, and as I was walking out, I was approached by this man. He was tall, had beautiful skin, green eyes, thick curly hair, and he smelled so good. He was smoking, so that was a turn off, but he was handsome and smooth. I asked him if he was married, and he said, "No!" He asked if he could take me to lunch, and I was like, "Maybe." Then, we exchanged numbers.

I had not seen him for a few weeks, so I pretty much forgot about him. One day, I was in my office, and we had a mail guy who brought us our mail. This day, I finally saw the guy I had met in front of my building bringing me my mail. In my mind, I was like, *there goes my caramel kiss*, and he was smelling so good. That was one of things I liked about him! I looked up and saw those beautiful green eyes and sexy smile and thought to myself, *DAMN*!

We hooked up that following weekend. It was the most romantic date I had ever been on (back then). He took me to a fancy restaurant, and we sat outside overlooking the ocean. The way he would look at me would make my heart melt. He fed me strawberries and ordered some delicious, sweet-tasting wine. He was so smooth to me.

He had a way with words. He would sweep me off my feet. We took a long walk around the pier, holding hands, laughing, and just having great conversation. It was a night I would remember.

I found out later that he was married. I went to lunch one day and saw this beautiful black woman with a white shirt, black skirt, black high heels, and a long ponytail. She ran up to him, gave him a package, and kissed him. I went back in the elevator. My heart dropped. It felt like the wind was knocked out of me. *How did I not notice the signs*? I had a number. I had been to his place, so I thought. He had my pictures up at his place. I could get in touch with him whenever I needed to. It did not make sense.

I saw him later that day, and I asked him who was the woman, and I described to him what

I saw. He admitted he was married, and he did not know how to tell me. He went on to say that they were not in a good place.

I was so hurt about this situation. I stopped seeing him for about a year because I never knew dating was this hard. I thought I would meet a guy and go on a couple of dates. If we liked each other, we would be exclusive. I would take a break from dating other guys because I wanted to remain faithful and hopeful that it would work out. I wanted to get married (at that time) and have a family like most people. Apparently, I was the only one thinking that.

Well, I had finally gotten a place with one of my co-workers, Isungi. She was such a positive influence in my life. She was God-fearing, and she loved to sing and go to church. She brought me back to the Lord's house. I knew I should have been in somebody's church. I was raised to go to church every Sunday to give God the praise for getting me through the week. I had forgotten how much I loved going to church. My mom used to say, "You will have a good life and a good week when you go to church and give God the praise for your life."

I started going back to church, singing in the choir, and attending Bible study. I even had my son going to children's church. I was trying to get my life back on track. One night, my church was having a lock-in for women. Basically, you go to church at night around 11 pm, and you do not leave until 6 am the next morning. We had several speakers who spoke about their life experiences. That was the best lock-in I had ever attended. It literally changed my life. I learned so much about womanhood at this lock-in.

We praised, cried, laughed, and talked. There was this one part that I will never forget. The pastor asked this young lady to come to the pulpit because she was crying so hard. They asked her why she was crying so hard. She said, "I can't let him go." The pastor asked, "Who can't you let go?" She said, "My boyfriend." The pastors, who were women, began praying over her and ministering to her. After they were finished, they told her that she was going to have to let that man leave out of her life. She told them she could not and walked back to her seat.

Later in life, I understood what she meant. We all have an addiction to someone or something. Some things are easy to let go, and some things are not. That is why we all need help at some point. I felt her when she said that. That hit me to my core. I knew exactly how she was feeling. I felt the same way about the married guy.

We all have been in situations where we know that someone or something is not good for us, yet, we still stay. Something in our minds and souls causes us to think that we do not deserve better, or that is as good as it gets. Unfortunately, we do not realize that we are blocking our blessing because we do not know how to let go of something that we know in our heart of hearts is not good for us.

So, why do we stay? We know why! For one, we have forgotten to see ourselves as God sees us. When we take our eyes off Him, the view of ourselves becomes distorted, and we tend to forget that we are fearfully and wonderfully made. When this kind of love eludes the fingertips of a man, we must gather our senses to rediscover and embrace our identity in the arms of God.

Now, my plant is drowning. I am over fed. I am getting the information I needed to become a better woman, but why haven't I gotten it? Let me show you what I am talking about.

"Everything that look good isn't always good for you."

Chapter 8

I KNOW BETTER

I broke off the relationship and started dating someone else. He was a nice guy. We had a great time together, and that lasted about a year.

I ran into the married guy, and he told me the marriage was over and asked if he could take me out. I remember that day like it was yesterday. It was a week before my birthday, January 5, 2000, to be exact. It was the craziest thing. I had butterflies in my stomach like I was a teenage girl going on her first date. I felt bad because I was feeling the other guy I was seeing. In my mind, I was going on this date just to see what he had to say. I was not falling for his smooth-talking self. I was going to get that free meal and to look good, so he would see what he was missing because I had a man.

I did not need him because he was a liar, a cheater, and I was not into him anymore. I was telling myself that because deep down inside I *was* still into him. There was a knock on the door. I opened the door. There he was looking like a caramel kiss with those green eyes. He was well dressed from head-to-toe and smelled like a bed of roses. Everything I said went out the window. Let us just say, we never made it out the house.

I got pregnant with my second son. I had to tell my current boyfriend I was pregnant – and it was not his child! He was so devastated because he really loved me. That was the biggest mistake I ever made, letting that man go. He wanted this baby to be his so bad, but I knew it was not his. Walking away from him was the hardest thing I had to do. That is who I should have been with. He treated me like a queen, even though we did not end up being together. I do not regret the time we spent together. He came in my life at the right time. He gave me a taste of how a man was supposed to treat a lady. I know hot mess, right?

So, here I go again – second baby – a different baby daddy. Here I was in another relationship that was not right. This man was married, and to top it off, his wife was pregnant, too. What in the hell did I get myself into?

I knew the decision I was making was wrong, but in my mind, I thought I was different, and I would be treated better. This was the beginning of my karma. I did not realize what I was putting in the universe. Baby, my plant was about to die, and I did not realize the harm that I was about to cause for so many people because of a choice I made in the moment.

Now, I was not only making poor choices about my life, but I was interfering in other people's lives. My roommate left. She had gotten her own place, so I had the apartment to myself. I finally got a car and was still working at my good job. To make matters worse, I worked with the man I was dating who was married, and now, I was pregnant by him. That is when I learned *you do not shit where you eat*.

He still had not left his wife, so now I was the mistress who was sneaking around with him. I knew I was wrong. I knew better than this. I was not raised to be this way. I could not blame this man. I allowed this to be done to me. I knew people were looking at me crazy, judging me, laughing at me, calling me names, and shaking their heads when they saw me.

I kept trying to make sense of a situation that I created for myself – thinking, *there was no turning back*." I could have walked anytime, but I did not want to have another failed relationship and another baby daddy. So, I thought to myself, *I will go through this humiliation for the sake of my child*.

As I look back, it was not worth the heartache and pain I went through to be in that toxic relationship. Do not get me wrong, we had our good days and bad days. I will say that relationship taught me that whether it is a man, woman, child, mother, father, or friend; no relationship is perfect. You must work at it, and you must work at it TOGETHER. I stayed in that relationship for 10 years, on and off. The only good things I got out of that relationship was life-learned lessons, my son, and Julie Wilson.

Julie is the ex-wife of my son's father. She and I became close over the 10 years. We were pregnant at the same time, with boys. Let me be clear: this was not how it started out. It was a long road to where we are today. We became friends because we both realized it was not about the man. It was about the kids. We both loved each other's boys like they were ours. We both had another son from a previous relationship, but you could not tell us that we did not have four kids together.

God is so funny. In my mess, there was a message. On this stage called life, I had to endure such things to grow and learn. At the time, Julie did not know she was the one who helped me define my purpose. Now, another seed was planted for womanhood. Clearly, I was not being a woman about anything. Being around Julie taught me integrity, accountability, loyalty, friendship, sisterhood, uplifting, self-love, honesty, mothering – and most of all – love for another woman. That helped me succeed beyond the impossible. Together, as a team, we did that!

By now, hopefully, you understand that my flower had another flower, and we were growing together. We sometimes needed some encouraging words from a sister who had our best interest at heart. That is called maturity, willing to learn to find myself, with an extra pair of leaves.

"A flower does not think of competing with the flower next to it. It just blooms."

Chapter 9

LATE IN THE MID-HOUR

It was all in God's plan how Julie and I became so close. One thing we knew about our kids' father was that he loved his boys, and he wanted to raise his boys together. So, Julie and I decided to deal with each other for the sake of the kids. We did not know we were forming this relationship called sisterhood, co-parenting, and friends. We were just doing what we had to do for our children.

We always knew, no matter what, they came first. We never talked about it. We started doing it. Dropping off the kids, changing uniforms in the car at the 7-11, the sleepovers, summer camps, afterschool activities, doctor appointments, birthdays, vacations, and school drop-offs. The list goes on.

Well, one day, we arrived at the kids' afterschool care at the same time. I was coming out the school, and she was coming in. Like always, we spoke to each other, "Hey Girl!" and kept on moving. But this day, I felt something in my spirit that was saying, "You need to apologize, and I promise it will set you free." I was like, "*Huh??!!!!*" (to myself). I had the kids in the car, and I sat in the car waiting for Julie to come out. I really struggled in my mind if this was something I wanted to do right then. Was I really prepared to hear what she had to say? Would I be able to handle her response? Because Julie did not sugarcoat anything! I knew that about her.

I realized in my mind, it was time to take accountability for my actions: put my big girl panties on and be a woman about it. I was bold enough to do it, so I had to own my stuff. She finally came out. I got out of the car and said, "Hey, Julie, can I speak with you for a moment?" She said, "Yes, girl, let me just put the kids in the car." She walked over to me, and I said, "I want to apologize for everything that has happened. I want to apologize for my part in destroying your marriage." She stated, "Ria, I forgave you a long time ago, and you did not destroy my marriage; it was already over. Your situation was the straw that broke the camel's back (She is amazing with her analogies may I add)." Believe me when I tell you, it felt like a load was lifted off me, and she went on to say, "I had to forgive you, not just for you, but for myself, so I can receive the blessings that God had for me." She continued, "Now, that I have forgiven you, you now have to forgive yourself."

Julie gave me validation to get rid of the guilt that I had been feeling for years. She set me free. I will forever be grateful to Julie. I thanked her so much, and we hugged, and we have been inseparable ever since. See, what y'all do not understand, there was a message in that mess. If I had not gone through that situation, I would not have met Julie. You see, what the devil made for bad, God made for good. That is why I say I would not change my journey because I would not have my son or my sister Julie!!!

From that day forward, we talked every day. We got together and hung with the kids. She would cook and bake for me and my kids all the time. I remember her telling me a while ago she never had my cooking. That is because I had a second job, so she would always cook for me and the boys before I went to my second job. Well, one evening, I was over a friend's house, and I was thinking about how ironic the relationship Julie and I had was. I thought about how I wanted to reach out to other women and share my journey, so they would not make the same mistakes I did. I felt if I had a group of women I could have gone to for advice, or if there was a place where I could have gotten some guidance, things would have turned out different for me. Nonetheless, I knew

I could not organize this by myself. A light went off in my head, and it said to ask Julie. My first instinct was, "Hell No!" That lady ain't about to do a whole non- profit with me. She was probably being cordial and may have not necessarily liked me like that.

I went to sleep that night, but something woke me up out of my sleep around 5 am and said, "Go to Julie's house." Now mind you, I had to be at work at 6:30 am at the time. I jumped up, went to Julie's house, and knocked on the door. It was 5:30 am. She opened the door, "Hey, is everything all right?" I said, "I'm so sorry, Julie. I need to talk to you." She was like, "Oh…ok, come in (wiping her face)." I said, "I want to start a non-profit organization for women, and I want you to do it with me." She looked at me with this shocked look on her face. She was like "Oh my God! Ria, I have for the past few months been wanting to do something like that but could not quite figure it out. When you said non-profit for women, my mind just clicked." She said, "Yes," and that was the birth of Sircles.

Sircles is a non-profit organization for women. We tried Circles with a C, but it was taken by the state. What was so ironic about it, Circles was for a breast cancer group. So, we changed it to an "S" for "Sisterhood." Then, we registered the name Sircles.

My flower was blooming. My garden was starting to fill up. I was going to help women to not go through what I had been through, so they could have a chance at a better life by not making the mistakes I made. Now, in my garden, I would be planting seeds in these women, so they could create their own garden. Julie and I were about to start saving lives together!

"Little girls with dreams become women with vision."

Chapter 10

THE BIRTH OF SIRCLES

Julie and I did not waste any time getting started. We met every week to build our empire. Julie oversaw the business part of Sircles, and I oversaw marketing. We worked well together.

At the very beginning of the business, we discussed our strengths and weaknesses, so we could determine, situationally speaking, who would make the best decisions for the organization. Our open house was in August 2007. Only six people showed up! We were a little disappointed, but we knew the show must go on, and we were going to do what we planned. It turned out to be so nice and fun. After that, we stepped up our game. A few meetings later, we had a location, staff, members, and a legit non-profit with a tax number to run our organization. We became so popular. We were motivational speakers at different churches, seminars, workshops, and events. We were promoting our business on radio, TV, and at colleges. Sircles changed my life forever. It was the first time in my life I thought of an idea and executed it with the help of my sister, Julie!

I remember we were invited to the Russ Parr Morning Show. It was a popular radio station in D.C. At the time, Russ Parr and friends were building a small community for domestic violence victims and their families. Domestic violence was one of the outreach initiatives that Sircles was very much involved in. Russ Parr noticed us and reached out to us to be a part of the project. We met so many people that day. I remember sitting at this long table in a board room. Julie and I were so excited. We had a personal assistant/sister/friend (Best one ever) called Nneka Crump. She went everywhere we went, and she did not play when it came to us. Each person had a chance to speak about what they did and what part we would play in this project. When he came to Julie and me, I completely froze and started crying. Julie had to do all the talking because I was so overwhelmed with my emotions. I remember that day so vividly. I was thinking, "I cannot believe we are on the Russ Parr Morning Show talking about Sircles." All the late nights we stayed up working on our website, cooking, running errands, decorating, and marketing for events had finally paid off. We were finally being recognized for the work we were doing. I completely lost it, and all I could remember, by the time it was over, was not much. I was over Tia's house (Julie's sister/our publicist, at the time) asleep on her couch in her basement because I cried so much. I fell asleep, and when I woke up I was hungry.

After that, we were really booming. We started having 30-40 women every month. We would get together and discuss different topics about what we as women go through daily. We had speakers come in. We would invite the men from time to time to join us. That was always fun. We did a domestic violence benefit gala. We had close to 100 people. It was simply amazing. People came from out of town and everywhere. I remember my proudest moment: when I walked Julie's grandmother, Mrs. Queen, in the building. My heart was so full, I finally met a woman that Julie love so much. To see the look on Julie's face when she saw her grandmother was priceless. It was the first time I saw Julie vulnerable, she looked like a little girl on Christmas day. I was glad to be a part of that moment for her. Julie is one of the strongest women I know. To know her is to love her. You must know her to understand this monumental moment.

Sircles taught me so much about sisterhood. Sircles was the foundation that prepared me for the next level in my life. We did different projects after that. My garden was beautiful with different flowers all through the field. I was planting my seeds, watering them, talking to them, and living my best life, professionally.

Personally, I was suffering. I failed yet another relationship. My kids' fathers were getting on my nerves because they were so involved in their lives (which was a good thing, sometimes). I became so unhappy in my personal life that I made a decision that would affect every single person around me, including my kids. I reconnected with a guy from the past and let him convince me to come back to Florida to start a life with him. That situation had so many red flags that I should be ashamed to talk about it. Because at this point in my life, I knew better–for real. I knew this was a bad idea, but I started making excuses when I realized it was a mistake. I felt, at the time, it was too late to turn back because I would really look stupid. So, I left everything I worked so hard to build, including relationships, partnerships, and my kids. I was in a dark place, but not knowing what I was going to get into was worse. I did not know how much more my poor garden could take. All these poor choices and decisions! I was over 30-years old. I knew better!

"Be the woman you needed as a girl."

Chapter 11

HOME IS WHERE THE HEART IS

I knew this was a bad decision, another failed relationship. I was not sure what I was looking for in a relationship, but I saw all the red flags with this one. I did not know why I continued to self-inflict pain on myself when it came to men. Maybe, I felt like I needed a man. In my mind, I was getting older, and I did not want to die alone. Well, this relationship was torture. He was one way over the phone, but in person, he was a monster. He was verbally and mentally abusive.

When I was going through that mess, I felt I was not being abused because I would talk and fight back. The last straw was when he decided he wanted two women at the same time. That would be a "NO" for me. I was not making good choices with men, but I did not want to share my man. To top it off, I lost everything I worked so hard for. I lost my job at Red Lobster where I worked for over 10 years. At the new Red Lobster, I worked for, the manager was prejudice. I had never experienced that in the workplace. I lost my place, was on the verge of losing my car, and was on my way back home. I had nowhere to stay. I had $75 in my pocket, but I had to get away from that toxic situation. I thought to myself, *I am going back home to where the heart is. I'm going to stay with my sister/cousin Nikki, but she doesn't know it yet."*

Things did not go as planned. I ended up staying with my aunt. She helped me find a place. I had three jobs, and my dad bought me a "cash" car to get around. I tell you; God is so good! Regardless of how many bad decisions I made, God always helped me and pulled me through. I give God the praise because everything I have been through some people could not have bounced back from. One thing I can say about myself, I was determined to make a life for myself and my kids. When I moved into my place, I did not have anything but my TV, clothes, shoes, and jewelry. I literally left that previous relationship with nothing.

Even with my poor decision of getting involved in that relationship, I knew when you leave a situation, and you want to progress, you leave EVERYTHING! So, here I was in the middle of the apartment with nothing, starting over, yet again. I knew this time I had to do the right things and use better judgement. I was getting too old to keep making the same mistakes. I could not keep starting over.

I worked my three jobs and furnished my whole place within a few months. I had made my house a happy home, again. My kids were still in DMV, but they came to visit for holidays. They had a place to stay when they came to visit. I was content being by myself.

Then, I met a tall, handsome, chocolate, and fine young man. My garden was coming back to life! The flowers were blooming and smelling nice. I think after a few failed relationships and poor decisions, I was actually seeing the light. I was so glad I came back home. I have no regrets. I went away and had a chance to experience the city life. Trust me, I loved the DMV! That was my second home. That was where I went from a young lady to a woman! I formed some of the best friendships that I will always cherish so dear to my heart. It was time for me to come home, and you will soon know why!

"Although the world is full of suffering it is also full of overcoming it."

Chapter 12

THE DIAGNOSIS

It was now 2017. Several years had passed! A lot had happened. I started my new business, Wine and Conversation. I moved to my new place, new job, new car – and I was still with the love of my life.

We have been dating for five years now – best relationship I have ever been in – hands down. Our relationship was not perfect, but it was perfect for us. I guess I should have gotten it by now!

My mom had just moved back from the DMV. Life was good! Me and my girls went to the Essence Festival, and we had a blast. It was a much-needed vacation.

One evening in August, I felt a lump. I asked my spouse to feel the lump, and he said,

"Oh yeah, I feel that, you may need to get checked." I waited a couple of weeks and got it checked out. I went to the doctor, and he asked me did breast cancer run in my family. I said, "No." He gave me antibiotics and said he would see me in seven days. Well, I came back in seven days, and the lump had gotten bigger! This time, he sent me to get a mammogram diagnostic, and they said I needed a sonogram. Then, I had to do an MRI! That is the devil! I hated that machine with a passion. Now, I was nervous because I was thinking I may have had breast cancer.

Why me, Lord!!! I was sick of always having to fight hard for everything or go through so much pain. They keep having me do all these tests. Well, the last test I had to take before I would find out if I had cancer or not was the biopsy. That procedure was very painful! My breasts were black, purple, and blue. Mind you, I do not bruise that easily, so that procedure was something serious.

After a few days, I received a phone call from my primary-care physician, and they told me I needed to schedule an appointment so we could talk about my results. I asked them if they could just tell me over the phone. They said, "No." I had to come in.

It was a day before Christmas, I asked, "Well, do I need to come in now." They said, "No, just enjoy your holiday, and we will see you after Christmas." I said, "Ok, thank you." I spent

Christmas with my dad and family. Afterwards, I went in the doctor's office. I checked in. Sitting and waiting for the results from the biopsy had me so nervous! I was crying before I even went to the back! Finally, they called me, and I went to the back. The doctor started talking to me like I knew what he was talking about, so I interrupted him and said, "Do I have breast cancer?" He said, "Oh, yes! I thought you knew."

The first thing that came to my mind was, "*I'm about to die.*" In that moment, I had so many thoughts that popped in my mind. *How am I gonna tell my kids, my parents, my family, my friends and most important the love of my life*? In my mind, I was planning my funeral, the color of my casket, the picture for my program and Brian McKnight singing at my services. I used to joke about that, but it did not seem so funny, now.

I did not even hear what the doctor was saying. He was sounding like Charlie Brown's teacher! Finally, after I got my thoughts together, I said, "I'm sorry. What did you say?" He went on to say I had Stage 3 Invasive Ductual Carcinoma, Triple Negative. The good news was that it did not spread to my lymph nodes or margins. I had no idea what he was talking about and was trying to process that I had breast cancer. He gave me a paper with a list of names on it and told me to pick one of the oncologists that he had circled on the paper. Then he said, "I'm sorry for your loss," and walked out the office.

I was so upset and scared I did not know what to do, so I went and sat in my car, looking at this paper he gave me. Then, I started to feel angry and was like, "My doctor is going to have to do better than this!" I needed to know what to do. I had never had breast cancer before. I needed him to tell me what to do, so I went back into that doctor's office and demanded to speak with my doctor. I told him I needed for him to tell me what to do. He looked at me and put his head down and apologized to me. Then, he told me what doctor to call and that he would help me going forward.

I got back in the car and called my sister. I did not get an answer, so I called my "Breastie," Monique, and I cried like a baby to her. She said, "Ok, we now know you have cancer. I'm going to give you a day to process what you heard from the doctor, but after that, you're going to need to get it together and fight." I said, "Ok."

Now, I needed to tell my spouse, kids, parents, family, and friends. I had even thought about not telling anyone because I did not want to hear all the "I'm so sorry's." "God is good." "He will bring you through it." "I'm praying for you." "It's going to work out," and "everything happens for a reason." I was not trying to hear any of that! I just wanted to wallow in my sorrow and feel sorry for myself.

Here came those thoughts, *I always get the bad stuff. This is my life, and nothing ever good happens to me. Everything I have gone through I had to work hard just to make it through. I guess this was my Karma for all the bad decisions I made.*

I was finally getting my life on track! Now, this began a new journey that I was not prepared for. A tornado had ripped through my garden, but everything was not destroyed. However, it would take a lot of tender love, care, water, patience, and help to get back to a blooming and beautiful garden, again.

I may have been a lot of things, but a quitter was not one of them! So, now I had to figure out where this journey was going to take me. Only God knew. For once in my life, I did not know what I was about to face. I was scared as hell!!!!!

"If you're always trying to be normal you will never know how amazing you can be."

Chapter 13

THE JOURNEY

I now had four doctors, and I had been given three options on how I wanted to do my treatment plan. The first option was to do radiation and chemo, and I could keep my breasts. The second option was to get the left breast removed, and still do chemo and radiation. The third option was to get both breasts removed and do four rounds of chemo.

The blessing was that I was going to live and not die. Praise the Lord! I had to make some life-changing decisions about my body and my future. I was so happy God had placed a beautiful black man in my life who said he would be by my side the whole journey. I remember asking him, "What should I do," and he was like, "I don't care what you do; it's your body. I just want you to be alive at the end of the day." So, I went with option three, remove both of my breasts and four rounds of chemo.

I selected that option because, at the time, I was 43, and my kids were grown, and I was not having any more children. It was a hard decision. People were like, "Oh, they're just breasts." Well, they have been my breasts for the last 43 years of my life, and I did not realize how much they meant to me until I had to have them removed.

My first surgery was February 2, 2017. They removed my breasts and replaced them with expanders. The expanders felt like two bricks were on my chest. I had to get my breasts pumped every week with saline solution. It was part of the reconstruction process for my new breasts.

I remember that day like it was yesterday. I had to take a test before the surgery because they wanted to make sure that the cancer had not spread to my lymph nodes and margins. Before I went back for that test, Monique and the Pastor showed up to support me. I was so happy to have their support. God was showing me favor in this journey, and I did not even know it.

That test was the worst I have ever had to take! I remember the nurse having to shoot dye in my breasts. He had that thick long needle. He said, "It is going to hurt, so I'm going to count to three, and I want you to breathe through it." He stuck that needle in my breasts, and I just knew I had stopped breathing for like 20 seconds! The nurse saw the look on my face. That pain hurt so bad that I could not react, so I held my breath thinking that the pain would go away quicker!

When the doctor saw the pain on my face, he screamed for me to breathe! That was a pain I had never felt before! I had two surgeons working on me that day. All my family and friends were there. They all came in to see me one-by-one, to kiss me, and to tell me they were praying for me. Kateria came up in there and said a prayer that even the nursing staff was like, "AMEN, we are ready to do this surgery." That was an amazing prayer! Then, the last person I saw before I went under was Bradford. I was about to cry because I was so scared, but he said, "I don't like no weak woman. You will be alright, and I'll be waiting for you." I held my tears in, and I got myself together and let them roll me in.

After the surgery, all my family and friends were there. They came in one-by-one and said their goodbyes because I was under a long time. I remember seeing my mom, Bradford, Nikki, Richard, Aunty Faye, Terri, Kateria, Latisha, Xavier, Katrina, and my Pastor. I was happy to see all of them in the shirts they had made for me. I remember thinking, "God, you didn't forget about me." I was back out like a light! That was some good medicine; I needed a thirty-day supply of that! I did ask the doctor, and he was like, "Ugh, no!" They said I had four to six weeks of recovery. Then, a few weeks later, I would have to start chemo.

I did not realize that God prepared me for this moment, and he was going to let me see my flowers while I was alive. I received so much love from New York all the way back down to Atlanta, Georgia. I received cards, money, gifts, food, desserts, and packages from Amazon. One of my favorite gifts was from Ms. Debra. I asked her for a Bible, and not only did she buy me a Bible, but she had my name engraved on it. All the years I thought God had forgotten about me, he let me see my blessings through my family and friends. I am so glad I knew God, because if I did not, I would not have been able to see Him work through my journey. He was all up and through my healing process. Hmm, I almost shouted while writing this!

Now, the first time I started chemo, that day was funny. I had tried to do what Monique and Mrs. Loretta said – to have an open mind and make sure I was cute. Well, I did all of that. But I remembered, when they administer the chemo, they go through a port. This port was located right above my left breast, and it was their first time using it. I was so nervous.

So, when the medication started, I thought I was having an allergic reaction to the medication because my left side started feeling numb. So, I ran to the nurse. "Oh my God, I think I'm having an allergic reaction. Please, help!" They responded, "No, just walk around and drink some water." My left side was going numb. I was so nervous I did not know what to do.

After the first round, I was ok until the next day. I was sick as a dog. I would feel cold one minute and hot the next. I would get sick for a week, and then when I would start feeling better, it would be time to take the next infusion.

After the second round of chemo, my hair started falling out. I woke up one morning and my hair was on the pillow. I could not believe how my hair was falling out. I could literally pull my hair and see the root where my hair was growing from. I remember feeling like why is this happening to me. I removed my breast to live, now my hair is coming out. How do I deal with this, everything that makes me feel like a woman was slowly being taken away from me? I know it is just hair, but it was mines. Why is this disease taking everything away from me that made me feel beautiful and sexy? What did I do that was so wrong, that I had to go through this type of torture?

I could not cry, so I went to my Aunty Faye's house. She is a barber and I got my hair cut off because I did not want this side effect, to affect me mentally. I decided I would just get this part of the journey over with. I went to my brother, Adam, to cut it all the way down. He was a barber, too. He was so proud of me for being such a trooper, but little did he know, I was a hot mess inside. My brother made me feel like a hero, that day he lifted my spirits, because he said, "Sis you got this". He never seemed too worried about me, but I get it now. He was not worried because he knew his big sis was strong, courageous, and he knew I would kick cancer's butt. I never told him thank you for helping me deal with losing my hair.

My mom was so amazing! She was on top of everything. She made sure I had everything I needed and wanted. If I could grow up to be half the woman she is, I would be a force to be reckoned with. I love my mom!

That whole journey lasted for about three months. It was the worst time of my life. I do not wish that part of my life on anybody! I was so happy when that part of my journey was over – May 23, 2017! Thank you, Jesus – a day I will never forget! I was cancer free! I could go back to being normal! Yeah, that is what I thought.

Yes, I am a Christian. Yes, I can be the biggest hypocrite ever. I backslide. I stumble. I fall. I stray onto the wrong path. But God is working in me. I may be a mess, but I am His mess and He is slowly straightening me out. And the day will come when I will be by his side, his work in me completed. Until that day I will take his hand and let him do in me whatever needs to be done, no matter how painful it will be for me. When he is finished, it will all be worth it.

Chapter 14

IT'S NOT OVER YET

I went to see my oncologist and he said my blood work was good, so he cleared me to go back to work. I was so excited to be getting back to some normalcy in my life. Bradford and I's relationship had gotten stronger, and I was going back to work the day after Father's Day. I was so excited to see my work family. I had not seen them in a year. I started going to counseling because I had some issues dealing with the fear of the cancer coming back, so I wanted to get control of my emotions and thoughts before they got the best of me.

I really enjoyed my counselors. They were amazing! I learned how to turn negatives into positives. They showed me how to reason with my thoughts when those negative vibes tried to creep in. I spent a lot of time at the Cancer Support Community Center. That place really helped me to adjust to my new normal.

Well, I was experiencing a lot of pain with those expanders. I was taking so much medication that I started to scare myself because I did not like being in pain; plus, I had to mentally prepare myself to go back to work. I had to get my expanders pumped every week for four weeks and that was painful. Once I finished that, I was able to go back to work.

I started back working knowing I was in all that pain. I worked for three months and had to go back out on short-term disability because I got an infection from the expanders. My surgery was supposed to be November 30th, but it was pushed back to December 4th. So, that was another Christmas ruined! I was so upset I cried for almost two days and did not let anybody see me go through that! I was so tired of this journey, and I was trying to remain positive. I just wanted things to go back to the way they used to be for me.

This was the second surgery, and it was a big one! The healing process for this surgery was different and harder. I had to learn how to sit up, roll over, walk, and get up without using my stomach muscles.

Taking showers was the hardest. I had four drainages this time which was so aggravating. I remember looking in the mirror crying. My body had so many scars and bruises. I could barely look at myself. I felt like I was dreaming. I realized I had been fighting for my life for two years.

I have experienced pain mentally and physically that I would not wish on my worst enemy. This whole process was exhaustive and was really taking a toll on me. Through all of this, I still had my support system. My family and friends were right there with me through everything.

My garden was still vibrant and even much stronger than before. I was already an overcomer. Although the emotional winds of life and hard-hit rains of adversity pelted upon my flowers, my vulnerable faith gave ear to the Master Gardener as He gently whispered into my spirit, "Hold on, just a little while longer. It is not over yet, but I will be with you, even unto the end of the world!

About the Author

Ria is a native of Sanford, Florida. She is a Wellness Coach, Motivational Speaker, and Co-Founder of Sircles. Ria is a Breast Cancer Survivor and she is the Founder of Wine and Conversation. Ria's purpose for creating Wine and Conversation was to lead men and women into conversations and steps towards the reinforcement of healthy relationships of all kinds. Everything is best spoken over a glass of wine.

After graduating from high school, she attended Prince George Community College, and subsequently transferred to Howard University to continue her studies as a Physical Therapy major. She has always had a passion to help those in the community. She was diagnosed with Stage 3 Breast Cancer in December 2017. She is now cancer free and a survivor of two years!

Ria turned her worse nightmare into a dream. She is now the Ambassador and Outreach Coordinator for a nonprofit organization called Pink Passion, "I'm my Sistah's Keeper". She motivates, encourages, uplifts, and educates women to get their mammograms, and with early detection they can survive this horrible disease. She also donates her time to Compassionate Hands and Hearts Breast Cancer outreach program, to help women who are going through treatment and currently diagnosed.

Life after cancer is hard, but Ria is alive and fighting to live her best life everyday with God on her side. She has two handsome young boys, Quenton (23) and Jaylen (19). She knows the struggle of a single parent household but was fortunate enough to have support from their fathers. After years of being frustrated, trying, and ending in a never-ending circle she discovered the key to achieving life's goals, positive and lasting relationships.

Acknowledgements

Thank you to my amazing Parents, Furman R. Clark, and Helena S. Clark for supporting me in everything I do. I love you to life. Without y'all there would be no me.

Thank you to my Bonus Mom, Pamela L Sharper-Clark, for stepping in to raise me. I know it was not always easy, but know I love you and thank you for your love and support. You are appreciated.

Thank you, Ms. Evelyn Dickerson for treating me like I was one of your children. I will always remember how you treated me through the years. I love you so much. I thank God every day for placing you in my life. You were so what I needed in my life. You were like a second mother to me. I pray for strength and health for you every day. You are the best grandmother to my son, Quenton. I love y'all relationship, and I always wanted that for my son. To have a grandmother that love him just as much as my grandmother love me.

Thank you to my brothers, Adam E. Clark, Brandon Clark, and Bradley Clark for your love and support. I love being your older and only sister, best title to have. Love sharing life with you. I am so proud of y'all!

Thank you to my Siscos (Sister/Cousin), Nicole Lemon Peterson and Terriashi Alexander for your love and support. For always encouraging me to achieve my dreams, never letting me get down about my life. Letting me know I am somebody and will do great things. Reminding me to never give up. Accepting me for all my flaws and never judging me but supporting me with truth and love. You are my world and cannot see life with you guys. I know I am the oldest, but I look up to you. You are my inspiration.

Thank you to my cousins, who always have my back and look out for me growing up into womanhood. We had some fun times growing up and I love you guys to life. Happy to be part of an amazing family!!!!! I would not have it any other way!!! Cherry, Scipio, Tillman, Livingston, and Clark

Thank you to my Aunts and Uncles for assisting my mom and dad to help create the woman I am today. Your guidance and knowledge has helped me through life even when I didn't make the best choices, but because of the advice you gave me growing up helped me to bounce back and never let anybody keep me down for long. Love y'all and I thank God for y'all every day.

Joyce, Anthony, Lawrence, Elijah, Margaret, Hilda, Faye, Larry, Cynthia Claudette, Carolyn, Ellen, Val, Tony, and Mannie

Thank you to my Best Friends and Sisters for life from my young days up until my adulthood. You ladies mean the world to me. I could not imagine life without you. You ladies taught me the meaning of friendship. Kateria, Latisha, Katrina, Xavier, LaKeisha, Dione, Julie, Nneka, Tina, Antoinese, Shanicka, Debreita, Latasha and Keishawn

A special thanks to all my friends who looked out for me through life and my breast cancer journey. You know who are and too many to name, but I will try. Renee, Paulinda, Celeste, Michelle, Tangela, Debra, Sheryl, Arlene, Kanesha, Brittany, Mattie, Keyah, Padricka, Tonya, Monique, Eboni, Sand, Hope, Kenya, Monica, Bianca, Michelle, Shelly, Lily, Barbara, Synsha, The Haynes Divas, Sanquita, Kristie, Tiffany, Lisa, Angie, Ashton, Shay, Melody, Sabrina, Paula, Gena, Trell, Bandi, Marsha, and Tammy.

Thank you for kind word, prayers, and gifts. You will forever be in my heart.

Thank you to my cuz/Brother-in-law Richard Peterson for editing my book. Always have a kind word to say to me, support me and gave me the best advice.

Thank you to my Beta writer and friend Ebony White for working with me to bring the best out of me to be vulnerable in this book. I so appreciate you from the bottom of my heart.

Last but not least the Love of my Life, my soul-mate, my best friend, my handsome chocolate bar, Bradford D. Newman, you are absolutely the best thing that has ever happened to me. I never knew there was a man that still exist that would be perfect for me. I cannot simply thank you enough for your love and support. You allow me to be myself and you love me through everything. Your love never changed. Thank you for completing me.

To my loved ones that are no longer here, may your souls continue to sleep in Paradise.

Psalm 91

1 Whoever dwells in the shelter of the Most High
   will rest in the shadow of the Almighty. [a]
2 I will say of the LORD, "He is my refuge and
my fortress,
   my God, in whom I trust."
3 Surely, he will save you
   from the fowler's snare
   and from the deadly pestilence.
4 He will cover you with his feathers,
   and under his wings you will find refuge.
   his faithfulness will be your shield and ram-
part.
5 You will not fear the terror of night,
   nor the arrow that flies by day,
6 nor the pestilence that stalks in the darkness,
   nor the plague that destroys at midday.
7 A thousand may fall at your side,
   ten thousand at your right hand,
   but it will not come near you.
8 You will only observe with your eyes
   and see the punishment of the wicked.
9 If you say, "The LORD is my refuge,"
   and you make the Most High your dwelling,
10 no harm will overtake you,
   no disaster will come near your tent.
11 For he will command his angels concerning
you
   to guard you in all your ways;
12 they will lift you up in their hands,

so that you will not strike your foot against a stone.

13 You will tread on the lion and the cobra;

you will trample the great lion and the serpent.

14 "Because he[b] loves me," says the LORD, "I will rescue him;

I will protect him, for he acknowledges my name.

15 He will call on me, and I will answer him;

I will be with him in trouble,

I will deliver him and honor him.

16 With long life I will satisfy him

and show him my salvation."

Made in the USA
Columbia, SC
05 September 2023

22482030R00076